80
COMMON
LAYOUT ERRORS
TO FLAG
When Proofreading
BOOK INTERIORS

LYNETTE M. SMITH

80 Common Layout Errors to Flag
When Proofreading Book Interiors
Lynette M. Smith

Disclaimer

This book provides guidance on the types of layout errors commonly encountered in the interior layout of a book before it is published and gives some idea as to techniques the layout professional may employ to remedy the errors. This is by no means an exhaustive list of all possible types of layout errors. *80 Common Layout Errors to Flag When Proofreading Book Interiors* is sold with the understanding that the publisher and author are not engaged in rendering professional book-design services. Furthermore, this book's content is based solely on the author's own experience during many years of conducting her copyediting and proofreading service. If expert assistance is sought that falls outside the scope of professional copyediting and proofreading, the services of a competent professional should be sought. Readers are solely responsible for their own choices, actions, and results and are therefore admonished to exercise good judgment when proofreading books. The author and All My Best shall be neither liable nor responsible to any person or entity with respect to any loss or damage caused, or alleged to have been caused, directly or indirectly, by the information contained herein.

Published by
All My Best
5852 Oak Meadow Drive, Yorba Linda, CA 92886
GoodWaysToWrite.com
Copyright © 2015 Lynette M. Smith

Print Book ISBN: 978-0-9858008-5-7
Kindle Ebook ISBN: 978-0-9858008-4-0
First Edition 2015

Contents

Introduction

What Does Proofreading *Really* Mean?

Proofreading **means checking a document that has already been laid out** (hopefully by a layout professional, also known as a graphic artist or graphic designer) to make sure it contains no last-minute content errors or layout errors. Proofreading usually means working with a printer-ready or duplication-ready PDF file, flagging the errors for the layout professional to correct. Other times it means working with an unbound galley proof from a traditional printer, or a sample bound print-on-demand (POD) book. Regardless of format, the printer-ready version of the book is being submitted to the author or professional proofreader for approval before being published and made available for sale or distribution.

The proofreader's role is vital for three reasons:

- Even the most meticulous copyeditors and authors miss occasional content errors when the document is sent out for professional layout.

- Layout professionals are artists; they don't read your manuscript, so they won't see these lingering content errors.

- Even excellent layout professionals make mistakes.

A professional proofreader flags both content errors and layout errors for the layout professional. The two of them collaborate on subsequent revisions, keeping the author in the loop, until both proofreader and author are satisfied that the layout and content are excellent and ready for printing and/or distribution.

Are you currently a professional proofreader or do you aspire to be one? *80 Common Layout Errors to Flag When Proofreading Book Interiors* offers excellent guidance for proofreading black-and-white book interiors.

Or are you a book author, wondering if you're capable of proofreading the layout of your own book? If you have a great eye for detail, aren't burnt out from reading your own writing multiple times already, feel you can address the layout with "fresh eyes," have the time and inclination, and are confident of your qualifications for the task, you may attempt it, and *80 Common Layout Errors to Flag When Proofreading Book Interiors* will help you. Note that this categorized list of 80 errors does not address the almost limitless types of grammar, punctuation, and spelling errors that may still be present—those have to be detected and flagged, too.

Not up to the task? Then hire a professional proofreader to assist you with this crucial stage of publishing. Editorial Freelancers Association is one good place to ask for help through their job postings; visit *The-EFA.org* for more information. Always check the experience levels and references of proofreaders who respond to your request for a quote.

Directions

Proofread the first layout in Phases 1 and 2. Proofread revised layouts in Phase 3. Repeat Phase 3 until all parties agree that the layout is acceptable and ready-to-publish.

PHASE 1 is performed while there are no flags (error notices) already in the layout, so nothing obscures or distracts from the overall layout of type on the page. In this phase, scrutinize—without actually reading—each single page or two-page spread in the PDF document or other proof copy. Watch for and flag the following described items:

- **Body text:**
  Inconsistent paragraph alignment *(Item 11)*;
  accidental inconsistency in fonts and font sizes
  (Item 14)

- **Block quotations:**
  Inconsistent left and right block indents
  (Item 18); inconsistent font size among block
  quotations—should be slightly smaller than
  body text *(Item 25)*

- **Numbered or bulleted lists:**
  Fully justified text—should be left justified
  (Item 26); right indent not the same as left
  indent for numbers or bullets *(Item 27)*;
  inconsistent left and right indents from one list
  to the next *(Item 28)*; inconsistent font size

within and among lists—should be slightly smaller than body text *(Item 29)*; inconsistent bullet style or size, within and among lists *(Item 31)*

- **Widows and orphans:**
  Only the first line of a paragraph (a widow), or a lone subheading, appears at the bottom of a page *(Item 33)*; orphan lines, in which only the last line of a paragraph appears at the top of a page *(Item 34)*

- **Certain types of end-of-line (EOL) hyphenations:**
  EOL-hyphenated word split between pages *(Item 36)*; EOL hyphenation at end of first line of a new page *(Item 37)*; EOL hyphenation on first or last line of a paragraph *(Item 38)*; EOL hyphenation on second-to-last line of a page *(Item 39)*

It may be more reliable to scroll or click through the page spreads, watching only for selected portions of the above items in each separate pass, until all listed areas have been scrutinized. Even when the Phase 1 proof-reading is complete in all respects, remain alert to those same issues during Phase 2 to detect anything that was overlooked the first time.

Note: In the item listings themselves, only those operations that begin in Phase 1 will be labeled.

PHASE 2 means reading the book one last time to flag any remaining copyediting or typographical errors, as well as the following categories of layout errors:

- Page Margins
- Headings and Subheadings
- Body Text
- Block Quotations
- Numbered and Bulleted Lists
- Widows and Orphans
- End-of-Line (EOL) Hyphenations
- Tables
- Figures, Including Photos
- Blank Pages
- Repeating Headers and Footers, Including Pagination
- Contents Listing

Each error type (item number) can be read in numerical sequence, or you can jump to a specific cluster of error types for more information.

PHASE 3 involves comparing the revised PDF layout or other revised proof copy to the flagged (error-marked) previous draft to make sure each error was corrected. In this process, any errors that remain are once again flagged, as are any new errors that become apparent in this process. No rereading of content is required other than in rewritten or recast text areas.

Phase 3 is repeated for each successive draft until both proofreader and author/publisher are satisfied that the PDF is as error free as humanly possible and the book is ready to be published.

Key to Point Sizes
And Their Height
Equivalents

The following table will be helpful as you read several of the listed items:

Point size	Inches		Centimeters	Single-spaced (12 point) lines	
	Decimal	Fraction	Decimal	Decimal	Fraction
1	0.014	1/72	0.035	0.125	1/8
3	0.042	1/24	0.106	0.250	1/4
6	0.083	1/12	0.212	0.500	1/2
12	0.167	1/6	0.423	1.000	1
18	0.250	1/4	0.635	1.500	1 1/2
24	0.330	1/3	0.847	2.000	2
36	0.500	1/2	1.270	3.000	3
72	1.000	1	2.540	6.000	6

For example, if the body-text style is full-block (flush-left) with 6 points of vertical white space between each paragraph of body text, that white-space gap is equivalent to 1/12 of an inch, or half (1/2) of a line.

80

COMMON
LAYOUT ERRORS
TO FLAG
When Proofreading
BOOK INTERIORS

PAGE MARGINS ~~~~~~~~~~~~~~~~~~~~~

1 Left and right margins not set up as "mirrored" to allow for wider bound edge. Even-numbered (left-facing) pages should have a wider right margin; odd-numbered (right-facing) pages should have a wider left margin.

2 Distance less than 0.5" between outer edge of page and either body text or repeating header or footer. Once the book edges are trimmed after printing, a small amount of this margin may be lost.

3 Distance less than 0.75" between bound edge and body text. A bound-edge margin of about 0.75" is recommended for a book that is 0.5" thick (about 250 pages or 125 physical pages printed back to back). That way, words near the bound-edge margin can still be easily read.

HEADINGS AND SUBHEADINGS ~~~~~~~~~

4 **Inconsistent font size and/or attribute(s) among chapter headings.** It's helpful to have a printout of the contents pages at hand when checking chapter and other major headings in the main body of the book, so the intended hierarchy is apparent. Jot down on the printout how a chapter heading should appear in the body of the book. For example, a note for a chapter-heading treatment might read "horiz. cntr. Garamond 22 pt bold title case" (where "title case" means capitalizing the first letter of the important words, as is done in a book title).

5 **Inconsistent white space above and below chapter headings.** All new chapters and equivalent major headings should begin the same distance from the top margin. The designer usually begins the chapter heading an inch (72 points) or two (144 points) below the top margin and might insert about 0.25" (18 points) of vertical white space below the chapter title.

6 **Inconsistent font size and/or attribute(s) among same-level subheadings.** Similar to what was done in Item 4, note on that same printout of the contents page how each subheading level should appear in the body of the book. For example, the most major subheading (Level 1) might be noted, "horiz. cntr. Arial 18 pt bold title case" (where "title case" means capitalizing the first letter of the important words, as is done in a book title); Level 2 might be noted, "flush-left Arial 14 pt bold title case"; and Level 3 might be "flush-left Garamond 12 pt bold sentence-case run-in w/text." In a "sentence case" subheading, only the first letter of the first word and proper nouns are capitalized, and the subheading ends in a period. "Run-in w/text" means that the subheading is followed, on the same line, by the first sentence of the body text, which, in this example, would probably also be Garamond.

7 **Inconsistent white space above and below same-level subheadings.** Sometimes the white space has been adjusted for page layout purposes, say, to allow an extra line of text to fit on the same page. Otherwise, the white space should appear the same for same-level subheadings. For example, a Level 1 subheading might have 18 points of white space above and 10 points below; a Level 2 might have 12 points of white space above and 6 points below; and a Level 3 might have 6 or 12 points of white space above and no space below, since it is run-in with the body text.

8 **Unwanted horizontal space or first-line indent before first character of left-aligned subheadings.** Quickly scan down the left margin of each page to assure that the text which is intended to be flush left truly is abutted to the left margin.

9 **Slight misalignment of centered chapter heading or subheading.** This can happen if, on that line, an unintended first-line paragraph indent was set, shifting the centered text slightly to the right of center. Or, in the original final manuscript draft given to the layout professional, some combination of tabs and spaces was used to try to manually center a line of text, rather than using the center-align command.

10 **Unwanted vertical white space above a subheading at the top of a page.** If a subheading occurs on the first line of a new page, it should be flush to the top margin.

BODY TEXT ~~~~~~~~~~~~~~~~~~~~~~~

11 Inconsistent paragraph alignment, e.g., ragged right margin when full-justified text is intended, or vice versa. Most professional book layouts use full-justified body text. However, indented block quotations, numbered lists, and bulleted lists often are intentionally left-justified (ragged right margin). *(Phase 1)*

12 Inconsistent or inappropriate vertical line spacing among blocks of text. Sometimes the line spacing within a given block of text on a page—whether body text or a list—has been discreetly adjusted to fill out a page or squeeze an extra line or two onto the same page. Otherwise, though, consistency in line spacing is the goal.

13 Accidental first-line paragraph indent in the first paragraph of a chapter or in the first paragraph following any subheading. In most—but by no means all—professionally produced books that employ a first-line paragraph indent for regular body text, flush-left style is still used for the first paragraph of a chapter or the first paragraph that follows a subheading or is run-in with a Level 3 (paragraph) subheading. Of course, a paragraph that begins with a drop cap is never indented.

14 Accidental inconsistency in body-text fonts and font sizes. Make sure body text that starts out as one font or size doesn't make a subtle switch to another in mid word, in mid paragraph, between paragraphs, or between subsections of the book. *(Phase 1)*

15 **Presence of two horizontal spaces between words or sentences.** Nearly all professional book layouts have just one space between sentences, not two. The two-space convention is a carryover from the old fixed-width-font typewriter days and is still used only in a rare few academic publications that have chosen not to adopt standard layout rules for proportional-width fonts.

16 **Too much white space between every word in a full-justified line, causing an unpleasant stretched look.** The layout professional can remedy this by using an end-of-line (EOL) hyphen in the first word on the next line (assuming that word has at least two syllables and at least two or three characters will appear on each line). However, if that stretched line occurs in the first line of a paragraph or in the second-to-last line of a paragraph, an EOL hyphenation should not be used. Instead, it may be possible to condense the character spacing in the stretched-out line plus the next word so the extra word will fit on the first line. Alternatively, the sentence can be recast (rewritten) slightly so the stretching will disappear.

BLOCK QUOTATIONS ~~~~~~~~~~~~~~~~

17 **Use of block quotations on passages of fewer than four lines.** Unless this is a horizontally centered famous quotation used at the beginning of a chapter, shorter quotations should be run-in with body text and surrounded by double quotation marks. If appropriate, insert transitionary language, for example, *He said, "Quotation."*

18 **Inconsistent left and right block indents for a given block quotation or from one block quotation to the next.** It's customary to block-indent the right margin as well as the left one, and by the same amount on each side, for example, 0.25" left and 0.25" right. All block quotations through the book must use these same indents, whatever it has been decided they should be. *(Phase 1)*

19 **Inconsistent white spacing preceding and following the block quotation.** Whereas one book layout may use only 6 points (half a line) of vertical white space above and below the quote, another layout may use up to 24 points (two lines) of vertical white space above and below. The amount of vertical white space preferred for this book layout should be the same at the top of the quote as at the bottom. However, a block quotation that starts at the top of a page should begin at the top margin, with no intervening white space.

20 **Fully justified text.** Ragged right margin (left justification) is normally used in block quotations.

21 **Overly ragged appearance of individual lines within the block quotation.** A reader can be distracted when a very short line follows a very long one, or vice versa. This excess raggedness can be minimized by adjusting character spacing, by using an end-of-line (EOL) hyphenation on a word (except on the first line or second-to-last line of a given paragraph within the quotation), or even by forcing an entire shorter word from the end of the longer line to the beginning of the next by using a nonbreaking space between them. (Layout programs have a provision for a nonbreaking space; so do word-processing programs on a PC—just type Shift–Control–Space Bar.) The last line of the quotation may be a short one, as long as it contains at least two words.

22 **Incorrect treatment of space (if any) between paragraphs of a given block quotation.** No vertical white space should be present between the paragraphs within a block quotation if subsequent paragraphs already have first-line indents.

23 **Accidental first-line paragraph indent on the first paragraph of block quotation.** Such a paragraph should have a first-line paragraph indent only if a first-line paragraph indent is also used in the regular body text, in the first paragraph following a chapter heading or subheading. (See also Item 13.)

24 **First-line paragraph indent on the second and subsequent paragraphs of a block quotation if flush-left paragraph style is used in regular body text.** Instead, a small amount (3 or 6 points) of vertical white space, used consistently, should appear between the flush-left paragraphs of the block quotation.

25 **Inconsistent font size within and among block quotations.** The font size for a block quotation is normally 0.5 point or 1 point smaller than regular body text, and the size should match that which is used for numbered and bulleted lists. *(Phase 1)*

NUMBERED AND BULLETED LISTS ~~~~~~

26 **Fully justified text.** In most books, a ragged right margin (left justification) is used in numbered and bulleted lists. All such lists should appear the same in this respect. *(Phase 1)*

27 **Right indent not indented to match left indent of number or bullet within a given list.** For example, if the numbers or bullets begin 0.25" from the left margin and the hanging indent is another 0.25" further, then the right indent for this list should be set at 0.25" (not 0" and not 0.5"). *(Phase 1)*

28 **Inconsistent left and right indents from one list to the next.** All numbered and bulleted lists should have uniform left and right indents. However, further left and right indenting is permitted for a second-level numbering system, such as an *a* and *b* beneath a numbered item or hollow bullets for a second-level bulleting system. *(Phase 1)*

29 **Inconsistent font size within and among numbered or bulleted lists.** The font size for numbered and bulleted lists is normally 0.5 point or 1 point smaller than regular body text and matches the font size used for block quotations. *(Phase 1)*

30 **Overly ragged appearance of individual lines within the list.** A reader can be distracted when a very short line follows a very long one, or vice versa. This excess raggedness can be minimized by adjusting character spacing, by using an end-of-line (EOL) hyphenation on a word (except on the first line or second-to-last line of a given listed item), or even forcing an entire shorter word from the end of the longer line to the beginning of the next by using a nonbreaking space between them. The last line of the listed item may be a short one, as long as it contains at least two words.

31 **Inconsistent bullet style or size, or inconsistent font size and attributes of numbers listed.** Consistency is the goal, not only within a given list, but also from one list to the next. *(Phase 1)*

32 **First or last listed item accidentally formatted as regular text, rather than numbered or bulleted.** Reading for comprehension during Phase 2 usually makes this type of error apparent.

WIDOWS AND ORPHANS ~~~~~~~~~~~~~~~

33 **Widow lines, in which only a lone subheading or the first line of a paragraph appears at the bottom of a page.** At least two lines of a paragraph must be present at the bottom of a page, and at least two lines of body text must appear on the same page as a subheading. One remedy is to force that line to the next page and optionally adjust the line spacing on that first page to fill out the page visually. Another remedy is to squeeze an extra line onto that first page, again, by adjusting the line spacing on that page. Yet another is to search for paragraphs on that page that can be rewritten slightly so as to occupy one less line, so the first two lines of the bottom paragraph will fit. *(Phase 1)*

34 **Orphan lines, in which only the last line of a paragraph appears at the top of a page.** At least two lines of a paragraph must be present at the top of a page. One remedy is to squeeze an extra line onto the previous page by slightly reducing its line spacing. Yet another is to search for paragraphs on that previous page that can be rewritten slightly so as to occupy either one line less than before or one line more so the last two lines of the bottom paragraph will be together on one page or the other. *(Phase 1)*

35 **Orphan words, in which only one word appears on the final line of a paragraph.** At least two words must appear on the last line of a paragraph. One remedy is to adjust character spacing to either squeeze the last word onto the previous line or use a nonbreaking space between the last word in the second-to-last line and the lone word in the last line so the two words will appear beside one another; or adjustments can be made in earlier lines of the paragraph, such expanding or condensing character spacing, using end-of-line hyphenations, or making minor rewrites that will favorably affect the last line.

END-OF-LINE (EOL) HYPHENATIONS ~~~~~

36 **EOL-hyphenated word split between pages.** Always end a page in a whole word. Remedies include adjusting character spacing or recasting sentence as needed. *(Phase 1)*

37 **EOL hyphenation at end of first line of a new page.** Always end the top line on a page with a whole word. Remedies include adjusting character spacing or recasting sentence as needed. *(Phase 1)*

38 **EOL hyphenation on the first or the last line of a paragraph.** Always end the first line and second-to-last line of a paragraph in a whole word. Remedies include adjusting character spacing or recasting sentence as needed. *(Phase 1)*

39 **EOL hyphenation on second-to-last line on a page.** Always end the second-to-last line on a page with a whole word. Remedies include adjusting character spacing or recasting sentence as needed. *(Phase 1)*

40 **Only one or two characters at end of one line or beginning of next in an EOL hyphenation.** At least two or three characters should appear on each line. Ideally, the author will have expressed a preference, before the layout is begun, as to whether at least three or at least two characters should appear on each portion of the EOL-hyphenated word. Any exceptions to that preference need to be flagged.

41 **EOL hyphenation of an already-hyphenated word.** Whereas *mass-trans-* / *portation central* (where "/" signifies the end of a line) is disallowed, *mass-* / *transportation central* is permitted, with the already-existing hyphen placed the end of the line. Remedies include adjusting character spacing or performing minor rewrites elsewhere in the paragraph that eliminate the EOL hyphen but not the regular hyphen.

42 **EOL hyphenation in which hyphen is improperly placed between syllables.** For example, *ordin-* / *arily* should be corrected to *ordi-* / *narily*. When in doubt as to whether a word has been divided correctly, use a dictionary or check *Webster's New World Speller/ Divider*, a valuable pocket guide available from brick-and-mortar bookstores and major online retailers.

43 **EOL hyphenation within a URL.** Never use an EOL hyphen in a URL, as the hyphen may be mistaken for part of the URL itself.

44 **Inappropriate division of a URL that continues on a second line.** Instead of using an EOL hyphen, consult the style manual being used by the author (for example, the *Chicago Manual of Style* or the *Publication Manual for the American Psychological Association*). In certain circumstances, these manuals may even suggest shortening the URL or using a digital object identifier (DOI) instead, assuming one exists.

TABLES ~~~~~~~~~~~~~~~~~~~~~~~~~

45 **Inadequate or inconsistent vertical white space above each table caption and below each table.** Ideally, this white space is equivalent to two blank lines, or 24 points, but the layout professional may need to vary this slightly for a given table to achieve a page-layout goal. Regardless, the amount of white space for a given table should be the same above the caption as at the bottom of the table.

46 **Inconsistent use of title case in table captions.** Table captions, always located above the table, require the same type of capitalization as a book title: initial caps on nouns, pronouns, verbs, adjectives (except *a*, *an*, and *the*, which are specialized adjectives called *articles*), adverbs, and interjections; on the first and last word of the caption; and optionally but consistently on longer prepositions such as *about* or *through*.

47 **Incorrect vertical white space between table caption and top of table.** The intervening vertical white space should be 12 points (1 blank line), unless spacing was adjusted for page-layout purposes.

48 **Misalignment of overall table within left and right page margins.** Even though not all tables may be the same width, they should be horizontally centered between left-and-right block indents of the same amount as used for numbered and bulleted lists. For example, if a full line of body text measures 4.75" and your standard block indents are 0.25" left and 0.25" right, then no table should exceed the remaining 4.25" width.

49 **Inconsistent table and cell border treatment from one table to the next.** Strive for consistency in every table for a unified look throughout the book. If the normal table style uses no vertical lines between columns, make no exceptions. If the top table border is 2.25 points thick, verify that every top table border is that same thickness.

50 **Inconsistency in font treatment within and among tables.** Use the same font within all tables. However, a smaller font *size* may be used to help fit copy within a crowded table. Or, if Arial or Helvetica is the font used within the table cells, Arial Narrow or Helvetica Narrow is a sufficiently compatible font to use for all contents of a crowded table.

51 **Poor vertical alignment of whole numbers and decimals from one row to the next within a column.** All whole numbers in a column should be right-aligned vertically. If there is a mix of whole and decimal numbers in the various cells of this column, the decimal portion should be vertically aligned to the right of the whole numbers.

52 **Poor horizontal centering of individual column headers or headers that span multiple columns.** A header that spans multiple columns should be horizontally centered over those columns. An individual column header—even for the left-hand column—should also be horizontally centered within the column.

53 **Inappropriate cell margins resulting in overcrowded or too-sparse cell contents or too much vertical space between rows.** Flag the columns, rows, or individual cells that need to be adjusted. Remedies may include changing cell margins or even changing a preset row height or column width.

54 **Inconsistent vertical alignment of cell contents within column headers and within all other cells.** Column headers must always be bottom-aligned. Row contents, with rare exception, are top-aligned. All top-aligned cell contents should have a uniform top margin in those cells, so they'll appear properly top-aligned when reading across a row.

55 **Inconsistent horizontal alignment of cell contents within column headers and within all other cells.** If a column requires a wide column header but contains narrow data below it, expand the left or right margin of the data cells so the data will appear nearer the horizontal center of the cell. For example, if this column of data cells consists of numbers from 1 to 999, expand the right cell margin of all the data cells in this column to 0.5" or 0.75", and then right-align the numbers against that newly expanded right margin.

56 **Cell contents positioned too close to left or right edge of column, so that the effect is not visually balanced.** While this is in one way similar to the previous error type, there is a subtle difference. It may be that the overall column width can be reduced. A long column header may be continued onto a second or even third line to permit narrowing of the column.

57 Full-justification of word-wrapped text within a cell. All narrative text within a cell should be left-aligned, with a ragged-right margin, as full justification of text within a limited space creates unsightly gaps between words.

FIGURES, INCLUDING PHOTOS ~~~~~~~~~

58 **Over-cropping, impairing completeness of graphic or legend.** The entire graphic subject needs to remain intact to communicate fully with the reader. The layout professional can usually work with the author to find or create a better image.

59 **Under-cropping outer edges of a figure, causing spacing issues.** White space on the four sides of a figure should be closely cropped to prevent too much space from throwing off vertical placement or horizontal centering between body text.

60 **Print within figure too small to read easily.** The average reader should be able to read all printing without the aid of a magnifying device. If a figure does not meet this criterion, the layout professional can query the author to see if the printing in the original graphic can be enlarged.

61 **Poor dot resolution, or "jagged edges," predictive of poor print quality.** The original graphic must be at least the width of the desired result; it can be reduced, but it should not be further enlarged. Images for a printed book should be at least 300 dots per inch, or 300 dpi. So the best-quality source for a graphic intended to be 4.25" wide should start out with at least 1,275 pixels wide (4.25" multiplied by 300 dpi). The layout professional should query the author to see if an appropriately larger graphic can be provided to replace the substandard one.

62 Poor photo treatment in terms of cropping, straightening, brightness, sharpness, or contrast. Good photo cropping shows the subject to the best advantage; when in doubt about cropping, the layout professional can query the author as to whether a given photo should be further cropped. Older photos may be crooked, faded, blurry, or lacking in contrast. In such instances, the layout professional can consult with the author for permission to modify the photo.

63 Use of color in an intentionally black-and-white/ grayscale layout. The layout professional should convert color graphics or photos to true grayscale before placing them in the layout.

64 Inadequate or inconsistent vertical white space above each figure and below each figure caption. Ideally, this white space is equivalent to two blank lines, or 24 points, but the layout professional may need to vary this slightly in a given figure to achieve a page-layout goal. Regardless, the amount of white space for a given figure should be the same above the figure as it is below the caption that appears at the bottom of the figure.

65 **Misalignment of overall figure within left and right page margins.** Even though figures may differ in width, make sure they're centered horizontally between left and right block indents of the same amount as used for numbered and bulleted lists. For example, in a 6" x 9" book, if a full line of body text measures 4.75" and the book's standard block indents are 0.25" left and 0.25" right, then no figure should exceed 4.25" in width.

66 **Inconsistent use of sentence case in figure captions.** Unlike table captions, figure captions appear below the figure. And also unlike table captions, figure captions imitate a sentence, rather than a book title. In a figure caption, the only words whose first letters are capitalized are the first word plus any proper nouns.

67 **Inconsistent font size and attributes among all figure captions.** The same font size, typically the same size as what's used in indented block quotations, should appear in every figure caption. Also, attributes such as italics should be uniformly applied from one figure to the next.

68 **Incorrect vertical white space between bottom of figure and caption.** The intervening vertical white space should be 12 points (1 blank line), unless spacing was adjusted for page-layout purposes.

69 **Duplication of figure title when caption already states the title.** This often occurs with charts and graphs. The recommendation is usually to have the layout professional crop out the internal figure title and then use the wording for the sentence-case figure caption at the bottom. If each of the two captions have different wording, everything should be incorporated into the longer figure caption at the bottom to retain clarity.

BLANK PAGES ~~~~~~~~~~~~~~~~~~~~~~

70 **Missing or unintended extra blank pages in front matter.** In the front matter, blank pages serve only to ensure that all front-matter elements, except the copyright page, begin on a right-facing page. Examine each page of the front matter carefully, and flag any blank pages that don't belong, as well as any other pages that will require a new blank page to be inserted immediately afterward.

71 **Missing or extra blank page before new chapter, depending upon design decision as to whether new chapters must begin on right-facing pages.** Most books are designed to begin each chapter or other major section on a right-facing (odd-numbered) page. Learn the layout professional and author's decision before judging whether blank pages before new chapters are appropriately placed and whether a blank page needs to be inserted before a new chapter. If the chapters of a book are grouped within major parts or sections, each with its own half-title page, such a page always begins on a right-facing page and is typically followed by a blank page.

72 **Missing or extra blank page after half-title pages for back-matter elements or before major elements in the back matter, depending upon design decision as to whether new elements must begin on right-facing pages.** Many variables exist here, depending on the design decision. One book may use a right-facing half-title page, followed by a blank page, to introduce each element such as the appendix, reference list, or index. Another book may use the same concept but skip the blank page following the half-title page, so the element itself starts on the left-facing (even-numbered) page following the half-title page. Yet another book may forgo the half-title pages and simply ensure that each element begins on a right-facing page by inserting a blank page, if needed, at the end of the preceding element. And still another may start each element on the next available page, whether left- or right-facing. Learn the intended design relating to blank pages before attempting to flag related errors.

REPEATING HEADERS AND FOOTERS, INCLUDING PAGINATION ~~~~~~~~~~

73 **Use of repeating header on first page of chapters and other major sections.** No repeating header, even if the header contains a page number, should print on the first page of a chapter or other major section. Note that this item applies only to repeating headers, not to repeating footers.

74 **Use of repeating header or footer on an otherwise blank page.** No repeating headers or footers should ever appear on otherwise blank pages.

75 **Appearance of page number on title page, inside title page, or dedication page.** Even though these pages count in the overall numbering sequence of Roman numerals, no page number whatsoever should be printed on them.

76 **Accidentally beginning a chapter or other major main-body or back-matter component on an even-numbered (left-facing) page.** Unless the author wants no blank pages in the book's main body or back matter, the first pages of chapters and other major book components should begin on odd-numbered (right-facing) pages. Be sure of the design decision before marking this as an error.

77 Wrong, duplicated, or out-of-sequence page numbers wherever page numbers are displayed. Whether in the front matter, body of the book, or back matter, blank pages always count in the sequence, even though no page number is ever printed there. The first page of the front matter, whether a title page or promotional page, counts as page i, in lowercase Roman numerals, and the sequence progresses from there. In some books, the introduction is considered part of the front matter and also is numbered in lowercase Roman numerals. In other books, the introduction is considered the first element of the main body of the book and is therefore counted as page 1, in Arabic numerals.

CONTENTS LISTING ~~~~~~~~~~~~~~~~~

78 Incorrect page-number callouts in the contents listing. Wait until one of the later revisions is being compared in Phase 3, and print a copy of the contents pages then. Compare the listed page numbers to the actual pages on which each listed element, section, chapter, or subheading begins, and indicate any needed page-number corrections. Later, in what's believed to be the final, clean, approved layout, make this comparison one last time, in case new discrepancies have crept in.

79 Missing headings or subheadings that should have been listed. If you are going to list the chapter subheadings in the contents listing for one chapter, do so for all of the chapters. And if you are listing, for example, two levels of subheadings in one chapter, you must do so for all other chapters, too.

80 Inconsistent treatment. Think of the contents listing as an outline with a clear hierarchy. Same-level entries should look the same in terms of font selection, size, and treatment (e.g., Garamond 12 point bold), line spacing, hanging indents on word-wrapped lines, decimal alignment of chapter numbers, and so on. In addition, the wording of the headings and subheadings shown in the contents listing should match exactly what appears in the rest of the book.

About the Author

Since 2004, Lynette M. Smith has operated the successful formatting, copyediting, and proofreading business, All My Best (*AllMyBest.com*). (Check out Lynette's Free Writing Tips—in plain English—published on her website.) She holds memberships in Editorial Freelancers Association, San Diego Professional Editors Network, Publishers & Writers of San Diego, and Publishers & Writers of Orange County.

Lynette also wrote and published the award-winning comprehensive reference book, *How to Write Heartfelt Letters to Treasure: For Special Occasions and Occasions Made Special,* available in softcover and ebook online; more information is also available from her publishing website, *GoodWaysToWrite.com.* Her Big, Achievable Goal is to get millions of people worldwide to write heartfelt letters of appreciation so they can establish, enhance, and even rebuild their relationships and in that way change their world.

Both personally and professionally, Lynette abides by the principles in *The Four Agreements* by don Miguel Ruiz:

> Be impeccable with your word.
>
> Don't take anything personally.
>
> Don't make assumptions.
>
> Always do your best.

Lynette can be reached through either of her websites or directly at *Lynette@AllMyBest.com* for matters relating to formatting, copyediting, or proofreading, or *Lynette@ GoodWaysToWrite.com* for matters relating to her Big, Achievable Goal and writing heartfelt letters.

Other Books and Resources
By the Author

INDIE PUBLISHING ~~~~~~~~~~~~~~~~~~

- *80 Common Layout Errors to Flag When Proofreading Book Interiors* is also available as a Kindle ebook from *Amazon.com*.

- *What Editors Do: Your Editorial Services GPS*. A downloadable PDF table that clarifies the different types of editors one might hire in the publishing process and the typical scope of work each type of editor provides, so you  won't waste hours, days, or weeks looking for the wrong kind of editor. Available only from *GoodWaysToWrite.com*.

- **Free Writing Tips in Plain English** regarding spelling; punctuation; word placement; word usage; clear, concise writing; and formatting. Click on Writing Tips at *AllMyBest.com*.

BUSINESS LETTER WRITING ~~~~~~~~~~~

- **Themed Letter-Writing Guides** extracted from the comprehensive reference book, *How to Write Heartfelt Letters to Treasure: For Special Occasions and Occasions Made Special* (9,000–11,000 words each). Each guide includes everything you need for writing a certain type of letter of appreciation. PDF at *GoodWaysToWrite.com*, print and ebook from *Amazon.com*. Choose from these titles:

  > ### *How to Write a Heartfelt Letter of Appreciation...*
  >
  > ♦ *To an Employee or Supervisor*
  > ♦ *To a Product Creator or Stellar Service Provider*

PERSONAL LETTER WRITING ~~~~~~~~~~

- *How to Write Heartfelt Letters to Treasure: For Special Occasions and Occasions Made Special* (55,000 words). Comprehensive, award-winning, reference book for writing 150 kinds of heartfelt letters of appreciation. Extensive appendix contains 15 demographic lists of positive words to describe someone special, famous quotations that can be included to start or end your letter, great beginnings to jumpstart your sentences, and much more. 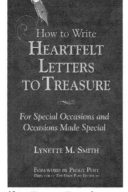 Endorsed by Peggy Post of The Emily Post Institute. Available in print and ebook from all major online retailers; signed or custom-inscribed printed copies available from *GoodWaysToWrite.com*.

- **Themed Letter-Writing Guides** extracted from the comprehensive reference book, *How to Write Heartfelt Letters to Treasure: For Special Occasions and Occasions Made Special* (10,000–14,000 words each). These comprehensive guides include everything you need for writing a certain type of letter of appreciation. PDF at *GoodWaysToWrite.com*, print and ebook from *Amazon.com*. Choose from these titles:

  ### *How to Write a Heartfelt Letter of Appreciation...*
  - ◆ *To an Older Friend or Relative*
  - ◆ *To a Military Service Member*
  - ◆ *For a Cultural or Religious Rite of Passage*
  - ◆ *To a Teacher, Coach, Mentor, or Student*

- **Marriage-Themed Letter-Writing Tips Booklets for Brides, Grooms, and Their Parents to Write to One Another** (3,600–3,900 words each). Create lasting gifts of appreciation! Available in PDF and print from *GoodWaysToWrite.com*:

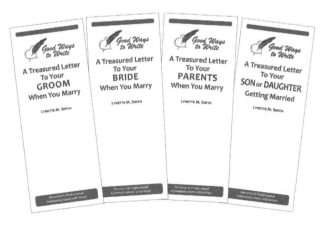

Printed in Great Britain
by Amazon